Painting & Decorating
BIRDHOUSES

Painting & Decorating
BIRD HOUSES

*22 step-by-step projects
to beautify your home
and garden*

Dorothy Egan

NORTH LIGHT BOOKS
CINCINNATI, OHIO

Painting and Decorating Birdhouses. Copyright © 1997 by Dorothy Egan. Manufactured in China. All rights reserved. No part of this book may be reproduced in any form or by any electronic or mechanical means including information storage and retrieval systems without permission in writing from the publisher, except by a reviewer, who may quote brief passages in a review. Published by North Light Books, an imprint of F&W Publications, Inc., 1507 Dana Avenue, Cincinnati, Ohio 45207. (800) 289-0963. First edition.

Other fine North Light Books are available from your local bookstore, art supply store or direct from the publisher.

04   03   02   01   00   9 8 7 6 5

Library of Congress Cataloging-in-Publication Data

Egan, Dorothy.
    Painting and decorating birdhouses / by Dorothy Egan.
        p.   cm.
    Includes index.
    ISBN 0-89134-737-2 (pb : alk. paper)
    1. Painting. 2. Decoration and ornament. 3. Birdhouses. I. Title.
TT385.E34   1997
690'.892—dc20   96-30348
                                                        CIP

Edited by Greg Albert and Jennifer Long
Designed by Sandy Kent

METRIC CONVERSION CHART

TO CONVERT	TO	MULTIPLY BY
Inches	Centimeters	2.54
Centimeters	Inches	0.4
Feet	Centimeters	30.5
Centimeters	Feet	0.03
Yards	Meters	0.9
Meters	Yards	1.1
Sq. Inches	Sq. Centimeters	6.45
Sq. Centimeters	Sq. Inches	0.16
Sq. Feet	Sq. Meters	0.09
Sq. Meters	Sq. Feet	10.8
Sq. Yards	Sq. Meters	0.8
Sq. Meters	Sq. Yards	1.2
Pounds	Kilograms	0.45
Kilograms	Pounds	2.2
Ounces	Grams	28.4
Grams	Ounces	0.04

ABOUT THE AUTHOR

Dorothy Egan has been involved with painting and the craft industry for most of her life. Her artistic career began as a matter of economy, as she restored old furniture and found creative ways to decorate her home on a newlywed's budget. Dorothy began to share her talents with friends and was soon earning extra money by selling her projects in consignment shops and at craft shows. After taking decorative painting classes, she began to teach at a local tole shop. Since then, Dorothy has produced or coproduced more than twenty-five books, is a regular contributor to several magazines, and has conducted painting seminars throughout the United States and Canada.

Table *of* Contents

Painting and Decorating Birdhouses

Introduction

*L*ong ago, Native Americans hung hollowed gourds to attract purple martins, realizing that having birds around decreased the insect population and thereby benefitted their crops. American colonists adopted this idea, constructing little houses and miniature mansions to entice helpful birds to build their nests nearby.

In the Victorian era, birdhouses were brought indoors to house exotic pet birds. Victorians undoubtedly found birdhouses a prime surface for elaborate decoration, and thus the purely ornamental birdhouse gained popularity.

With today's resurgence of environmental consciousness, people are once again attracted to the natural world. Realizing the therapeutic value of watching birds from a kitchen window or deck, as well as the benefits of natural pest control, birdhouses are popping up in gardens and yards all over the country.

Birdhouses have also become a major interior decorating trend, bringing the tranquility and charm of nature into the home. In fact, most birdhouses are built and decorated to satisfy a human need to create art and are never intended to be used by live birds.

This book is a one-stop source of information on products and techniques that can be used to paint and decorate premade birdhouses, including both functional and purely decorative projects. The decorative techniques given can be easily adapted to any style of birdhouse, whether premade or hand-built, and several projects include instructions for adding simple cuts of wood to generic birdhouses to create charming, unique designs.

It is my hope that with this material on hand, you will be inspired to let your imagination flow freely, experiencing the fun and satisfaction of creating a small work of art. ❧

Getting Started

This section will provide you with all the basic information you'll need to get started on your first birdhouse, as well as with some general hints to remember throughout the book.

Preparation

Since the steps involved in preparing a birdhouse for decoration vary little from one project to the next, basic preparation techniques and materials will not be repeated in each project, but rather described in depth in this section. Any variations from these steps will be noted in the project.

Filling Holes

To achieve a smooth, undimpled surface, you may choose to fill nail depressions and uneven areas with a commercial wood filler. Apply the filler with a putty or painting knife, slightly overfilling the hole. Allow the filler to dry according to the manufacturer's instructions, then sand the project as described on page 11.

page 11

Preparation Materials

- commercial wood filler
- small putty or painting knife
- sandpaper, sanding block or palm sander
- wood rasp (optional)
- tack cloth
- sealer (optional)
- large, flat, synthetic or sponge brush

Fill nail holes with wood filler and allow to dry.

Sanding

Most commercial birdhouses will need to be spot sanded, as shipping and changing climates will cause the grain to rise and curl. Several methods of sanding will produce the same basic result. Using plain sandpaper is very inexpensive and effective. Begin with a medium grit to remove the roughest spots, and then use a fine or extra-fine grit for the final sanding. Sanding blocks are also available, which are easier to hold and therefore make the job a little faster. A small, handheld vibrating sander, called a palm sander, is probably the quickest and easiest way to prepare the house for painting, but it's also the most expensive if you don't already own this tool. Sand rough surfaces with the grain of the wood, paying special attention to splintered or rough edges.

Use a sanding block, sandpaper or electric sander to remove rough spots and sharp edges.

A small electric palm sander is easy to use and makes quick work of smoothing the wood and removing sharp edges.

Aging

To create a primitive, well-worn look, use a wood rasp or one of the sanding methods to round squared corners and soften edges. A project can also be sanded after it's painted, to remove paint from edges and areas that would receive the most wear, heightening the aged effect.

Wiping With a Tack Cloth

Any time you sand a project, wipe the surface well with a tack cloth to remove all dust particles. A tack cloth is a treated cloth with a slight stickiness that picks up fine dust particles. Dust on the surface will make the finished piece rough and the paint may not adhere properly. Tack cloths are available where paints are sold.

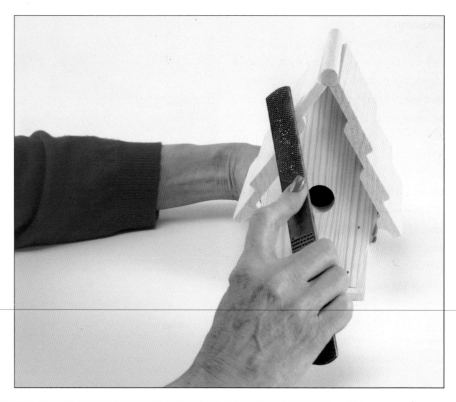

Using a wood rasp along the corners creates irregular, worn-looking edges for primitive pieces.

Wipe clean with a tack cloth after sanding.

Sealing

At this point you may wish to seal the wood. Although basecoating a project with paint is often sufficient to seal the wood, using a commercial sealer first makes painting easier and further protects the wood if the house will be used outdoors. Wood that will be stained rather than painted should be sealed first, as the stain will be easier to apply after sealing. The stain will be absorbed more evenly because end cuts and open grain won't "grab" the stain.

Many good sealers are on the market. If you are in doubt about what to use, ask your local paint dealer to recommend one. The projects in this book were sealed with Designs from the Heart sealer, which is available in most craft stores. Sealing the wood may cause some grains to curl up—when dry, sand again lightly, and wipe with a tack cloth.

Basecoating

Basecoating means to apply a smooth, even coat of paint over an entire surface. This paint will act as the

Apply wood sealer with a small piece of cloth, sponge brush or 1″ synthetic brush.

background for further decorative work. Remember that several light coats are better than one heavy coat.

The projects in this book are painted with bottled acrylic paints. Acrylics are an excellent choice because they come in a great variety of colors, are readily available, are easy to

use, clean up with soap and water, and are very durable. The brands and colors listed for each project are only suggestions—if you don't have a color listed, use the photographs to choose or mix a similar color. Colors can also be changed to fit your personal taste or decorating decor.

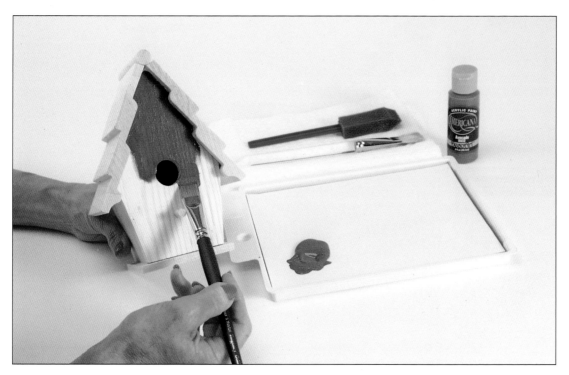

Apply the basecoat evenly with a 1″ synthetic or sponge brush.

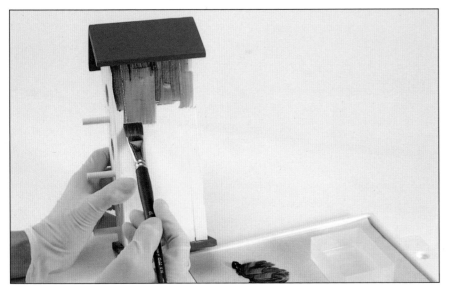

Apply thinned oil, acrylic paints or commercially prepared glazes to the surface of the birdhouse with a brush.

The surface should be completely covered with the antiquing glaze.

Antiquing

Antiquing is the process of adding a glaze of brown or black paint over a finished surface to produce an aged, slightly dulled effect. Although antiquing is suggested for some projects, you may decide you like the brighter, newer look of undulled paint and choose not to antique, or you may prefer to antique all of your projects to add a "historical" character. Since antiquing is a matter of personal preference, complete instructions and materials are listed in this section rather than within each project.

There are several methods of antiquing. The houses in this book were done with oil paints thinned with a few drops of odor-free thinner. Oils are inexpensive and versatile, because several colors can be mixed together to create a glaze that is just right for the base color used. For example, Burnt Umber may be too red in tone and Raw Umber too brown, but if they are mixed together, they make a warm, neutral antiquing color. Burnt Umber and black is another good combination. These oil colors can also be used as a wood stain.

Acrylics can be thinned with gel or blending medium to create a glaze, al-

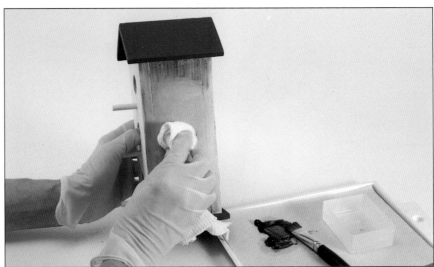

Wipe away excess antiquing with a soft, dry cloth.

Antiquing Materials

- oil paints, such as Raw Umber, Burnt Umber, Raw Sienna and/or black
- odorless thinner
- *or* commercial antiquing glaze
- *or* acrylic paint in above colors and a blending medium
- flat synthetic brush
- soft, lint-free cloth
- small flat brush
- commercial varnish

Painting and Decorating Birdhouses

though it is harder to achieve even coverage with this method. Premixed oil- and water-based glazes are also available in craft stores, paint stores and home improvement departments.

Antique after the entire project is painted and dry. A light coat of varnish will make the glaze easier to control and make it easier to create a soft, even effect. Applying the glaze to an unvarnished piece will result in a heavier, more rustic effect. Apply the glaze with a brush, then wipe away excess with a soft, lint-free cloth, wiping in a circular motion to prevent lines and streaks. Use a soft, dry brush to remove glaze from hard-to-reach places. Wipe with a soft cloth or brush dampened with thinner to remove more glaze for a more subtle effect or to create areas of highlight. Antiquing should be allowed to dry thoroughly before the final finish is applied.

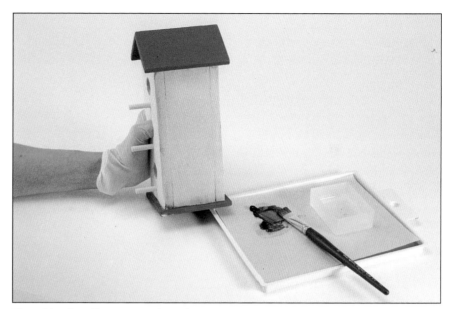

If you like the effect you've achieved, stop here and allow the glaze to dry.

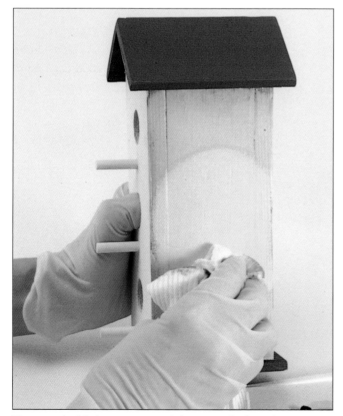

To create highlights or a very subtle antiqued effect, dip the cloth into thinner and rub the surface to remove more glaze.

Use a small brush to apply and remove antiquing in hard-to-reach places.

Varnishing

Finish your birdhouse with a good quality varnish, using a wide flat brush or sponge brush. Where you plan to display the house will determine the type of varnish used. A house that is purely decorative could be finished with a water-based brush-on varnish, while one that will be used outdoors would need to be finished with a product especially formulated for indoor/outdoor use. Read labels or consult your local paint store for advice.

Spray varnishes are another option. They are easy to use and require no brush cleaning but are considerably more expensive if you plan to do several birdhouses. Apply spray varnish outdoors. Hold the surface to be sprayed horizontally to prevent runs and the can several inches away to achieve a light, even mist. Several thin coats are better than one heavy coat. Be sure to cover all the areas of the birdhouse.

Other Finishes

Many other finishing techniques are used in this book, such as crackling, texturing and spattering, which can be applied to any style of birdhouse and used in any project. Experiment with these techniques to create a birdhouse that is very personally yours.

Wrong way

Right way

Painting and Decorating Birdhouses

Transferring a Pattern

Several of the projects in this book include an actual-size black-and-white pattern. Use these patterns as a guideline to freehand the designs on your project, or transfer the pattern directly to your surface. To transfer a pattern, lay a piece of tracing paper directly on the pattern and trace over it with a black pen. Flip the tracing paper face-down and trace over the back of the design with pencil or chalk, using a color that will show over your basecoat or surface color. Then position your pattern face-up on your project, and trace the pen lines with a stylus or dried-out ballpoint pen, which will transfer the chalk or pencil pattern onto the surface.

Locating Raw Birdhouses

Commercial preassembled, ready-to-decorate birdhouses are widely available at craft and hobby stores. Flea and craft markets are another good source of premade birdhouses, often providing unique shapes and personalized designs. Those with woodworking skills will enjoy building their own birdhouses to decorate. If you are unable to locate the style of birdhouse you need for any of the following projects, see page 126 for a complete list of the suppliers used in this book.

Brushes

Use a good quality brush or sponge brush. Many inexpensive synthetic brushes are available that wear well and are designed for decorative painting. The brush sizes listed in the instructions are guidelines—a larger or smaller size may feel more comfortable to you.

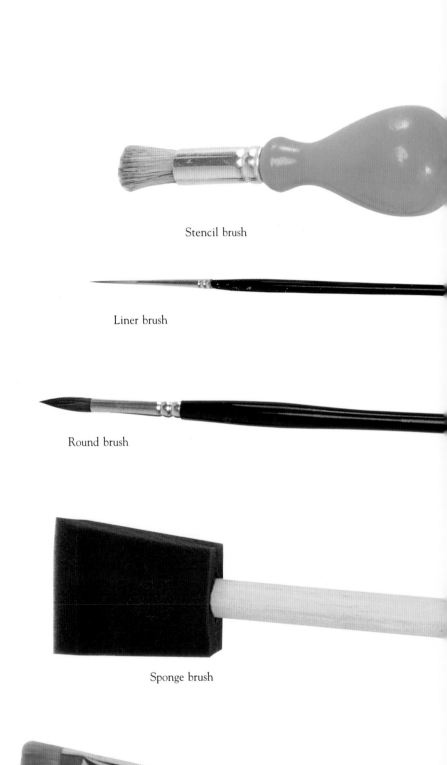

Stencil brush

Liner brush

Round brush

Sponge brush

Flat brush

P olka dots, checkerboards and stripes make this birdhouse a bit of whimsy and a lot of fun. This is an excellent first project, covering every step in detail, from sanding to finishing. It covers simple techniques even "non-painters" will be able to use, plus some that can be used on later projects in this book or on your own creations.

Paint the
Whimsical Polka-Dot Birdhouse

Materials

- craft store birdhouse

DecoArt Americana acrylic paints
- Titanium White
- Lamp Black
- Williamsburg Blue
- Boysenberry Pink
- Alizarin Crimson
- Cadmium Yellow
- Avocado

Brushes
- 1″ synthetic flat or 1″ sponge
- no. 2 flat
- no. 1 liner
- no. 6 round
- stiff bristle brush or old toothbrush

Miscellaneous
- kitchen sponge
- scissors
- pencil
- palette
- water container

1 Preparing the Surface.
Slightly overfill all nail holes and any imperfections with wood filler, allow to dry, then sand smooth. Sand the birdhouse well using one of the methods described on page 11, removing sharp corner edges and rough spots. Wipe with a tack cloth to remove dust particles. Apply one coat of wood sealer, let dry, then sand lightly with extra-fine-grit sandpaper. Wipe clean with a tack cloth.

Sanded and sealed house.

2 Basecoating.

Use a 1″ flat brush or sponge brush to basecoat the roof, eaves and base white. Basecoat the sides of the house black. Be sure to wash your brush or sponge thoroughly when changing colors. Let dry.

Use a ½″ or 1″ brush to basecoat the roof and base with white acrylic paint.

Basecoat the sides of the house with black.

Painting and Decorating Birdhouses

3 Painting the Trim.

Paint over the basecoat on the base, roof edges and trim with a thin coat of Cadmium Yellow. Allow to dry, then paint over any mistakes with the appropriate base color.

4 Lettering.

Write "Welcome" lightly with a pencil above the opening, adjusting the spacing if needed. Thin a little Williamsburg Blue to a creamy but not runny consistency by adding a drop or two of water. Use a liner brush to paint over the pencil pattern.

5 Adding Polka Dots.

To make the polka dots, squeeze a small amount of white onto your palette. Dip the handle end of a brush in the paint, then touch the end to the side of the house to make a dot. Refill the handle tip after one or two dots. You may wish to practice this on a scrap piece of paper first, to be sure you get the size of dots you want.

To make polka dots, dip the handle end of the brush into a small puddle of white paint.

Touch the end of the brush to the side of the house to make a dot.

Painting and Decorating Birdhouses

6 Sponging.

To make the checkerboard design on the roof, cut a scant 1″ square out of a kitchen sponge. Wet the sponge with water, then squeeze as dry as possible. To ensure proper placement of your rows, place the sponge on the top left corner of the roof and mark the side lightly with a pencil. Move the sponge over one square-length, and make another mark. Continue until the top row is marked. Squeeze a small amount of Williamsburg Blue onto your palette. Dip the sponge in the paint, then pat it on the palette to remove excess and distribute the paint evenly over the surface of the sponge. Place the sponge on the first square on the roof and press gently. Using too much pressure will result in a dark, blotchy square. Lift the sponge off the surface and rotate it once to the right. This ensures a varied pattern of holes in your sponging. Skip the next square, and press the sponge in the third square. When the first row is completed, sponge alternate squares on the second row, skipping the first square and sponging in the second. Continue, refilling and blotting the sponge as needed, until the checkerboard pattern is complete.

Dip a 1″ square of sponge into Williamsburg Blue. Pat it several times on the palette to remove excess paint and distribute color evenly over the sponge.

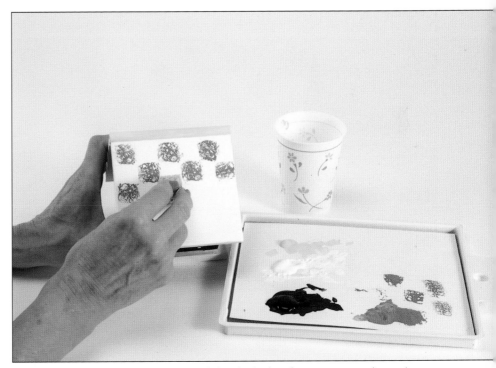

Continue sponging alternate squares until the checkerboard pattern covers the roof.

7 Painting the Stripes.
Use the no. 2 brush to paint narrow stripes around the yellow base with Alizarin Crimson.

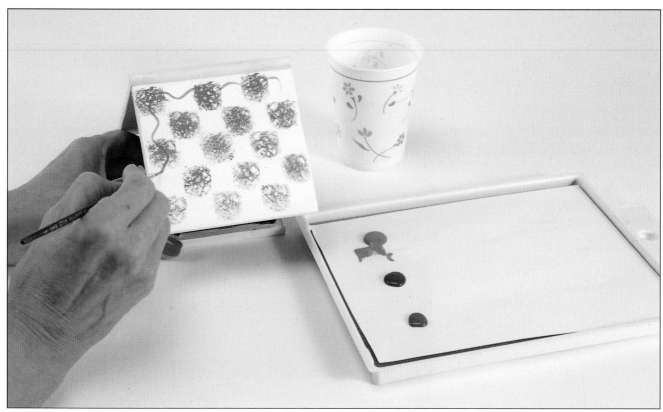

8 Painting the Border.
Use slightly thinned Boysenberry Pink on a liner brush to paint a border of wavy lines just inside the edge of the roof, connecting the lines at each corner.

Painting and Decorating Birdhouses

Paint the basic shape of the rose on the roof with thinned Boysenberry Pink.

9 Painting the Roses.

To paint the strokework roses, use the round brush to basecoat the basic circle shape of the rose with thinned Boysenberry Pink. Darken a small oval at the top center of the circle with Alizarin Crimson. This will be the throat of the rose. To create the shadow side of the rose, paint curving comma stroke petals with thick Boysenberry Pink.

To create a highlight side, repeat the last step on the opposite side of the rose with white, alternating the tails of the white comma strokes with the Boysenberry Pink ones. Paint varying sizes of comma stroke leaves on either side of the roses with Avocado. Add two small oval rosebuds with Boysenberry Pink, highlighting them with a stroke of white.

Basic rose shape and throat.

Darken an oval center at the top of the rose with Alizarin Crimson. Pull comma stroke petals on the shadow side of the rose with Boysenberry Pink.

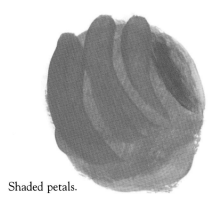

Shaded petals.

Pull comma stroke petals on the highlight side with Titanium White.

Finished rose.

Paint comma stroke leaves with Avocado. Add two buds with Boysenberry Pink, highlighted with white.

Painting and Decorating Birdhouses

10 Spattering.

To spatter the house, squeeze Lamp Black onto the palette. Dip a stiff bristle brush (such as a stencil brush or toothbrush) into water, then into black. Hold the brush approximately 6″ from the house, and pull a painting knife gently across the bristles toward you. You may wish to test this technique over newspaper if you've never done it before. The amount of water and the distance you hold the brush from the house will affect the size of the spatters.

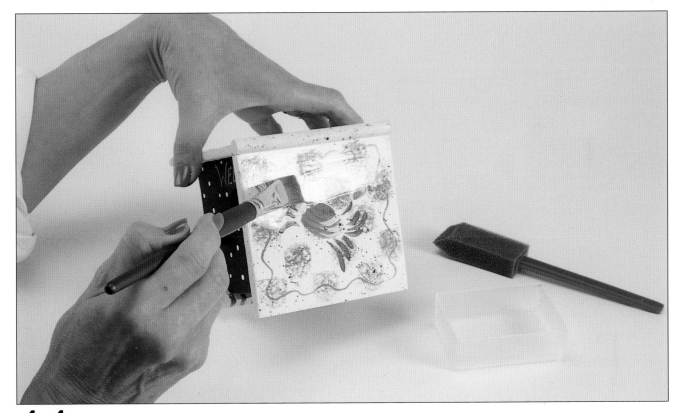

11 Varnishing.

When the paint has completely dried, finish the birdhouse with the varnish of your choice. See the "Getting Started" section for more about varnishes.

T he unique shapes and sizes of gourds may inspire many creative variations on this project. Gourds can be homegrown from seed or purchased at craft fairs, flea markets or farmer's markets. Most craft stores also carry papier-mâché gourds, which are a good substitute for the real thing if you intend to display your gourd indoors.

Paint the
Strawberry Gourd Birdhouse

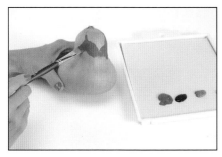

Basecoat around the leaf shapes with Pure Red.

Materials

- strawberry-shaped gourd

Accent Country Colors acrylic paints
- Pure Red
- True Green
- Pure Yellow
- Light Yellow Green
- Pine Needle Green
- Real Black

Brushes
- ½" synthetic flat
- no. 4 flat
- no. 1 liner
- small round detail

Miscellaneous
- pencil
- 19-gauge wire
- wire cutters
- drill with ¹⁄₁₆" bit
- hole saw
- bleach
- steel wool
- palette
- water container

1 Preparing Dried Gourds.
After homegrown gourds are thoroughly dried, the outer skin needs to be removed. Soak the gourd in water to which a little bleach has been added until you can scrape away the loose skin. Scrub the gourd with a stiff brush and/or steel wool. Allow the gourd to dry completely before painting.

Use a hole saw to cut a 1¼" hole on the front face of the gourd. No perch is necessary, because birds attracted to gourd houses will fly directly into the opening. Purchased gourds have usually been cleaned, and most vendors will drill the hole for you. (If you are only planning to paint one or two gourd birdhouses, this is definitely the easiest way to go. They are inexpensive to buy, and all the hard work has been done.)

Drill holes in the top of the gourd with a ¹⁄₁₆" bit. Insert 19-gauge wire in these holes before painting so you can hang the gourd to dry between coats. If the gourd has rough spots and small holes, fill the holes with wood filler and, when dry, sand the gourd well.

2 Basecoating.
Sketch three large leaf shapes at the top of the gourd. Use the ½" brush to paint the gourd Pure Red, working around the leaf shapes. Two or three coats may be needed for good cover-age. Let dry, then paint the leaf areas with True Green.

3 Painting the Seeds.
When dry, use a pointed round detail brush loaded with Real Black to paint seeds randomly around the gourd, spacing them ¾ of an inch to 1 inch apart. Highlight each seed with a stroke of Pure Yellow.

4 Painting the Leaves.
Use a liner brush with Pine Needle Green to paint veins on the leaves. Highlight the veins with Light Yellow Green. Allow to dry and varnish.

Paint the leaves True Green, vein with Pine Needle Green and highlight with Light Yellow Green. The seeds are painted with Real Black and highlighted with Pure Yellow strokes.

Complete with its own white picket fence and miniature birdhouses, this pretty pastel cottage will bring you visions of spring year-round.

Painting and Decorating Birdhouses

Paint the Spring Cottage Birdhouse

1 Building the Fence and Miniature Birdhouses.

Cut basswood or craft sticks into eight fence slats and six thicker fence posts. Create two L-shaped sections, using wood glue to crisscross two slats between each set of posts, as shown in the photo at left. When dry, glue the fence sections to the birdhouse base. To create the miniature birdhouses, cut molding into appropriate sizes to form a sloped box or triangle. Drill a ⅛″ hole in the center of both the front piece and the bottom piece before gluing the houses together. Glue the end of the dowel rod into the drilled hole in the bottom of the birdhouse.

2 Basecoating.

Sand the birdhouse lightly and wipe with a tack cloth to remove dust particles. Basecoat the house and chimney with Taffy Cream. Paint the roof, inside the opening and the base with Moon Yellow. Paint the fence and dowel rods Titanium White. Paint the roof of one miniature house with Green Mist and the other with Gooseberry Pink. Add a touch of the roof color to white to paint the sides of the miniature houses.

3 Painting the Flowers.

With the corner of a no. 8 brush, dab Holly Green and Pansy Lavender around the base of the house. When dry, squeeze Iridescent Light Green directly from the tube to make dots and flower stems. Use a spring variety of fabric paint colors for the flower petals, such as light blue, pale pink, pearly white, gold, lavender and turquoise. Lightly pencil in scrollwork on the front of the house under the eaves, and trace over it with the tube of Iridescent Light Green.

4 Finishing.

Varnish the entire house, fence and miniature birdhouses. Drill two ⅛″ holes into the base and/or fence post to mount the birdhouses. Squeeze a drop of glue into each hole and insert the dowel rods.

To create the flowers, dab Pansy Lavender and Holly Green around the base, pull up stems of Iridescent Light Green, and create dot blooms and leaves with fabric paints.

Birdhouses with a crackled finish are not weatherproof, so this house is embellished with silk flowers and ribbon to make it a beautiful indoor accent piece. This project includes instructions for two crackling techniques, one using hide glue (available at hardware stores) and the other using a commercial crackle medium. The crackled finish techniques shown here can be used on any decorative project you wish to give a primitive look, and can be done in almost any combination of colors as long as there is enough contrast between the top and bottom color so that the crackling shows to its best advantage.

Paint the
Crackled Victorian Birdhouse

To use craft store products such as Weathered Wood, apply an even coat of crackle medium and let dry according to manufacturer's directions.

To use hide glue as a crackling medium, squeeze it directly onto the surface you wish to crackle, then spread it as evenly as possible with a brush.

1 Basecoating.
Fill holes, sand the birdhouse lightly and wipe with a tack cloth to remove dust particles. Using a 1″ brush, basecoat the entire house with Raspberry. This will be the color that shows through when the topcoat cracks. Allow to dry.

2 Applying a Crackle Medium.
Use a flat synthetic brush to apply Weathered Wood, or a similar craft store crackle medium, to all surfaces. Set aside until dry to the touch, about twenty to sixty minutes. Skip to step 4. If you wish to use hide glue, simply skip step 2. All other steps are the same for both techniques.

3 Applying Hide Glue.
Squeeze a generous amount of hide glue directly onto the birdhouse, then smooth it with a brush until all surfaces are covered evenly. Set aside until dry to the touch.

Materials
• craft store birdhouse
• DecoArt Americana Weathered Wood medium
• *or* Titebond Franklin Hide Glue

DecoArt Americana acrylic paints
- Raspberry
- Buttermilk

Brushes
- 1″ synthetic flat or 1″ sponge
- no. 8 flat synthetic

Miscellaneous
- silk flowers
- wired ribbon
- two small decorative birds
- hot glue gun and glue sticks
- palette
- water container

4 Topcoating.

Paint over the entire house with Buttermilk. Use a thicker layer of paint to create larger cracks, as shown on the side of the house. Try to cover each area with only one or two strokes. Going over an area repeatedly may actually cover over forming crackles or lift paint, leaving an obvious blank spot on your surface. Stroke your brush up and down to create longer, vertical crackles.

Apply your topcoat in a thinner layer to achieve a finer, more delicate crackled appearance, as shown on the roof. Brushing the paint in all directions will create shorter, more squared, random crackles. Allow to dry thoroughly before sealing.

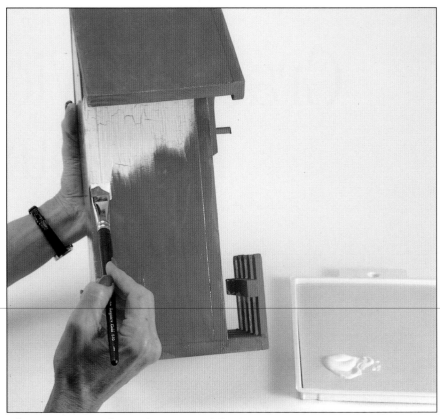

A heavy top coat results in a larger, more defined crackled pattern.

Using long, up-and-down brushstrokes to apply the top coat results in a vertical crackling pattern.

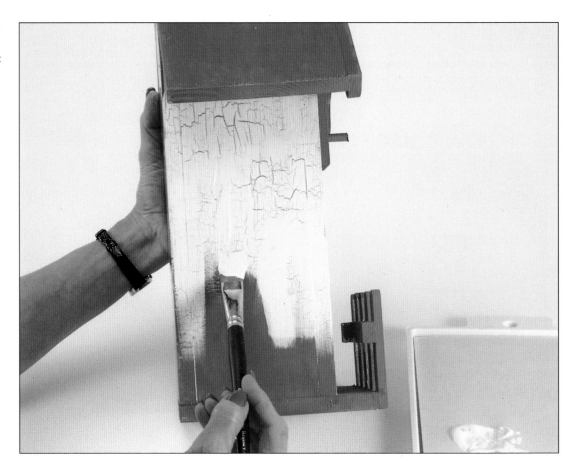

Painting and Decorating Birdhouses

For a subtle, more delicate crackled pattern, apply a thinner top coat.

Pulling brushstrokes in all directions creates a random crackling pattern.

5 Trimming.

Embellish the house with the trimmings of your choice, attaching them with a hot glue gun. Elaborate silk flowers give your birdhouse an elegant air. Wired ribbon is also a good choice, as it will hold its shape once arranged and is available in a multitude of colors and sizes. Available in most craft stores, tiny artificial birds are a perfect final touch for your decorative birdhouse.

right
Almost any color combination can be used for a crackled finish project. This birdhouse was basecoated with Heritage Green and overcoated with Pale Mint Green. For added interest, the colors were reversed for the roof.

The large, vertical pattern on the base was caused by a heavy top coat applied with vertical brushstrokes. The smaller, more delicate pattern on the roof resulted from using less paint and random brushstrokes.

Paint the Crackled Victorian Birdhouse

The delicate floral vines entwining this birdhouse may look intricate, but they are actually very easy to create. Perfect for a patio or a little girl's room, this design can be painted in any color scheme or adapted to fit any style of birdhouse.

Floral Strokework Birdhouse

1 Basecoating.

Sand the house well and wipe with a tack cloth to remove dust particles. Basecoat the sides of the house with Jade Green and the base and roof with Light Buttermilk. Let dry.

2 Painting the Front.

To paint the vines and flowers on the front of the house, use the liner brush to draw vine shapes with Forest Green. Add leaves and tendrils with Forest Green and Olive Green. Use Eggshell on a dry-wiped stencil brush to make soft, irregular dots for the flower centers. Use a liner brush loaded with Pure Red to pull tiny comma strokes from the tip of the petal toward the center. Press firmly at the tip of the petal, releasing pressure as you near the center. Make approximately half of the petals for each flower. Use a mixture of Pure Red and Light Buttermilk to make the remaining comma stroke petals. Make a few similar shapes with Forest Green. Use the handle end of the brush to place random dots of Light Buttermilk into the green areas.

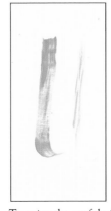 

To paint the roof design, use Jade Green on the flat edge of your brush to paint a wide stripe, then use the chisel edge to draw a line next to it. Paint the strokework flowers as shown.

3 Painting the Roof.

To paint the flowers on the roof, use Jade Green on the flat edge of a no. 6 or no. 8 flat brush to draw a wide stripe for the base of the floral design. Use the chisel edge to make a line ½" from the stripe. Repeat the vines, flowers and leaves from the front of the house. When dry, finish with the varnish of your choice.

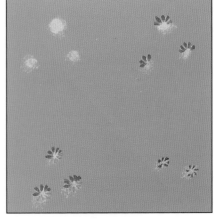

To paint strokework flowers on the front and roof, use Eggshell on a dry stencil brush to create centers. Paint half the comma stroke petals with Pure Red and half with Pure Red mixed with white or Light Buttermilk. Do the same with Forest Green.

Materials
• craft store birdhouse
DecoArt Americana acrylic paints
• Light Buttermilk
• Jade Green
• Pure Red
• Eggshell
• Forest Green
• Olive Green
Brushes
• 1" synthetic flat or 1" sponge
• no. 6 or no. 8 flat
• no. 1 liner
• ¼" stencil
Miscellaneous
• palette
• water container

There are schools of fish, so why not a schoolhouse for the birds? This super-easy project would make a great gift for favorite teachers, not to mention your neighborhood birds. Most craft stores carry this schoolhouse, or a similar version.

Paint the
Schoolhouse Birdhouse

Use thinned Slate Grey on a liner brush to paint broken lines over the pencil marks.

Use Slate Grey on a dry-wiped brush to pull feathery strokes up from the shingle lines.

1 Basecoating.

Sand and wipe with a tack cloth. Use a 1″ brush to basecoat all sides of the birdhouse, including the bell tower, with Country Red. Basecoat the roof and bell tower top with Lamp Black. Paint the base of the birdhouse with Slate Grey. Allow to dry.

2 Adding Details.

Using the picture at left as a guide, draw the door, windows and opening in the bell tower with a pencil and ruler, then paint them with Lamp Black. Paint the shutters and trim on the door and windows with Titanium White. Create steps by shading with Lamp Black above each step and on each side of the stairs. Load your liner brush with slightly thinned white for the lettering and hash marks on the windows. Paint the bell and doorknob with True Ochre, adding highlights with Cadmium Yellow and shading with Raw Sienna.

3 Adding Shingles.

To paint the shingles, divide the roof with horizontal pencil lines. Use the liner brush with Slate Grey to paint broken lines along the pencil marks. Now load a no. 10 brush with Slate Grey, wiping excess paint from the brush until it's "dry." Use the flat of the brush to pull upward strokes from the shingle lines, lifting the brush as you reach the next row. When dry, seal the entire surface.

4 Attaching the Flag.

Drill a hole for the flagpole in the base of the house. Paint the wooden dowel rod Slate Grey. Remove a paper flag from its stick, or paint one of your own, then glue it to the dowel rod. Finally, squeeze a drop of glue into the drilled hole and insert the end of the dowel rod.

Materials

- schoolhouse-style birdhouse

DecoArt Americana acrylic paints
- Country Red
- Lamp Black
- Titanium White
- Slate Grey
- True Ochre
- Raw Sienna
- Cadmium Yellow

Brushes
- 1″ synthetic flat or 1″ sponge
- no. 4 flat
- no. 10 flat
- no. 1 liner

Miscellaneous
- ⅛″ dowel rod
- paper flag
- drill with ⅛″ bit
- glue
- pencil
- ruler
- palette
- water container

B irdhouses that are decorative rather than functional can be made of a wide variety of materials. This project uses a papier-mâché teapot and paper napkins to create a birdhouse perfect for a kitchen shelf or cozy den. Look around your local craft store for other decorative ideas.

Painting and Decorating Birdhouses

Paint the
Teapot Birdhouse

Materials

- craft store papier-mâché teapot
- Mod Podge Gloss Medium
- decorative paper napkins

DecoArt Americana acrylic paints
- French Grey/Blue
- Uniform Blue
- Red Iron Oxide
- Golden Straw
- Desert Turquoise
- Hauser Green Dark
- Burgundy Rose
- Titanium White

Delta Ceramcoat acrylic paints
- Ultra Blue
- Fuchsia
- Lavender

Brushes
- 1″ synthetic flat or 1″ sponge
- no. 4 flat
- no. 8 flat synthetic
- fine liner

Miscellaneous
- ¼″ wood dowel, 2″ long
- scissors
- kitchen sponge or natural sea sponge
- craft knife
- white craft glue
- palette
- water container

1 Cutting an Opening.
Cut a 1¼″ hole in the front face of the teapot with the craft knife. Cut or drill a ¼″ hole below it for the perch.

2 Basecoating.
Paint your teapot and dowel rod perch in colors to match your napkin pattern. When mixing colors, remember that acrylic paints darken in value as they dry. If you are in doubt about matching a color, paint a sample on cardboard or poster board and allow it to dry. The sample project was basecoated with a mixture of Ultra Blue and Lavender with a touch of French Grey/Blue. Allow the basecoat to dry thoroughly.

Basecoat the teapot with acrylic paint to match or complement the napkin colors.

3 Sponging.

Wet the sponge with water and squeeze dry. Pull the corners of the sponge up so that the sponge forms a rounded pouf with no straight edges or corners. Dip the sponge into paint and pat it on the palette several times to remove excess paint and distribute color evenly. Lightly sponge paint onto the surface, randomly dipping into other colors and repeating until the surface is evenly sponged. Ultra Blue, Uniform Blue and French Grey/ Blue were used to sponge the sample project.

When sponging with more than one color of paint, do not clean the sponge between colors.

Start in one small area and apply all of the colors before moving on to the next section.

Painting and Decorating Birdhouses

4 Decoupaging.

Cut the design area you wish to use out of the napkin. Separate the napkin ply, using only the top layer that carries the design. Apply Mod Podge in a liberal but even coat to the area of the teapot that will be covered with the design. Carefully lay the trimmed design over the Mod Podge, and pat it gently to flatten creases and folds. Rounded surfaces will require the napkin to be pleated slightly as it is glued on.

Apply Mod Podge in a generous but even coat to the area that will be covered with the napkin.

Lay the trimmed design over the Mod Podge and pat it gently to flatten creases and folds.

5 Finishing the Decoupage.

If your napkin design covers the opening on the face of the teapot, clip the napkin over the opening so that it folds back inside the hole. Use Mod Podge to glue it in place inside the teapot. When the entire design is applied, gently brush over the tissue with another layer of Mod Podge, being careful not to tear the design. When dry, insert the perch and glue it in place with white craft glue.

6 Painting the Trim.

If you wish to add a painted design, choose a simple element from the napkin's design and lightly sketch it in a repeating border around the lid and knob. The sample lid was painted with Golden Straw shaded with Red Iron Oxide and detailed with Hauser Green Dark. Paint detail with fine liner brush.

The knob was painted with Fuchsia darkened at the bottom with Burgundy Rose and detailed with Desert Turquoise and Titanium White.

To create more interest, trim the knob with another element of the napkin's design.

7 Sealing.

When the trim is dry, paint the entire teapot with another coat of Mod Podge to seal it and create an even gloss finish.

Like the Crackled Victorian Birdhouse, projects that have been distressed, such as this Primitive Sunflower Birdhouse, are meant for indoor display only. The birdhouse pictured here is simply an old fence post, enhanced with a few accessories. However, if you live in midtown Manhattan, old fence posts can be hard to find. Here's a quick way to age a new piece of wood so it has that wonderful timeworn, weather-beaten look that's so popular today.

Painting and Decorating Birdhouses

Paint the Primitive Sunflower Birdhouse

Create gouges with a screwdriver, ice pick, nails or a wood rasp.

Use coarse sandpaper to remove paint from the corners and areas that would receive the most wear.

1 Basecoating.
To create an aged look, use a wood rasp to wear down square corners and soften edge lines as described on page 12 of "Getting Started." Mix black and off-white into a medium-value gray to basecoat the house lightly. When dry, apply an uneven coat of off-white, allowing areas of gray to bleed through. Paint the roof slate blue and the heart and perch barn red.

Materials

- craft store birdhouse

Any brand of acrylic paints
- black
- off-white
- barn red
- slate blue

Brushes
- 1″ synthetic flat or 1″ sponge
- no. 4 flat
- no. 1 liner

Miscellaneous
- screwdriver or other blunt tool
- hammer
- heart-shaped wooden cutout
- large silklike sunflower and leaves
- dried broom weed or straw
- Spanish moss
- wood glue or hot glue gun and glue sticks
- palette
- water container

2 Distressing.
To further age the wood, hammer the point of a screwdriver, ice pick or other blunt instrument into the wood, creating dents and gouges. Sand over the painted surfaces to create a worn, weathered look, especially concentrating on edges and areas that would receive the most wear. If the sanded areas look too new, wipe them lightly with wood stain or an antiquing glaze.

3 Adding Details.
Paint the lettering with a liner brush loaded with thinned black. Attach the heart cutout with wood glue or a glue gun. Seal the entire project, then use the glue gun to attach the Spanish moss, straw, leaves and sunflower. Refer to the photo at left for placement.

Decorated in red and green for Christmas, or with bright candy colors to be used year-round, these gingerbread birdhouses look good enough to eat! Use caulking compound or structural paint to create the white "icing"—both are weather-proof and can handle the outdoors. Create one or both projects, or intermix and use the gridwork pattern with the caulking compound and vice versa. Real gingerbread houses in cookbooks and magazines are a great source for decorating ideas to re-create on your birdhouse.

Paint the
Gingerbread Birdhouses

Basecoat the house with Raw Sienna or Tumbleweed.

Caulking Compound

1 Basecoating.
Sand the birdhouse lightly and wipe with a tack cloth to remove dust particles. Basecoat the entire house with Tumbleweed. Allow to dry.

Materials for the Caulking Compound Technique

- craft store birdhouse
- white caulking compound

Accent Country Colors acrylic paints
- Tumbleweed
- Pure Red
- Forest Green
- New Leaf
- Pure Yellow
- Dijon Gold

Brushes
- 1" synthetic flat or 1" sponge
- no. 1 liner

Miscellaneous
- small cake decorating tip (no. 3 - no. 7)
- butter knife or spatula or caulking gun
- pastry paper or plastic freezer bag
- scissors
- pencil
- small piece of sponge
- palette
- water container

Materials for the Structural Paint Technique

- craft store birdhouse

Liquitex Structural Paint
- TitaniumWhite
- Structural Brown
- Hooker's Green Hue
- Permanent Green Light
- Ivory Black
- Naphthol Crimson

DecoArt Americana acrylic paints
- Raw Sienna
- Cadmium Yellow

Brushes
- 1" synthetic flat or 1" sponge
- no. 2 synthetic flat

Miscellaneous
- glue injectors
- pencil
- ruler
- palette
- water container

2 Painting the Windows.

Wet a sponge and squeeze dry. Dip the sponge in Dijon Gold and pat several times on the palette to remove excess paint. Sponge window areas with Dijon Gold, then Pure Red. Do not overblend.

3 Caulking the Scallops.

Roll pastry paper into a cone and drop the pastry tip into the opening, or cut the corner off of a plastic freezer bag and insert a pastry tip in the hole. Use a caulking gun to squeeze caulking into the bag, or cut off the wide end of the caulking tube and use a butter knife or spatula to transfer the compound to the pastry paper or bag. Draw the first rows of roof scallops lightly with a pencil to check for spacing. Squeeze the compound through the decorating tip along the pencil lines. After the caulking dries slightly, use a fingertip to flatten loose ends.

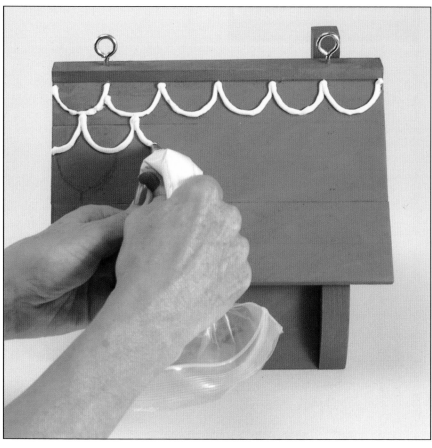

Painting and Decorating Birdhouses

4 Caulking Details.

Use the caulking compound to draw window frames and scrollwork on the front of the house, using the photo on page 50 as a guide. Make a brick design on the chimney. To make connected dot trim along the side edges, squeeze out a drop of the compound, lift the tube, then move to the next space and squeeze again. Repeat until all edges are covered. Squeeze round dots on the sides for the flowers.

5 Painting Details.

When the caulking is dry to the touch, use the liner brush to paint stems and leaves for the flowers with Forest Green and New Leaf. Paint the flowers Pure Red, let dry, then add Pure Yellow centers. Caulking should be allowed to dry and cure for several days. Varnish.

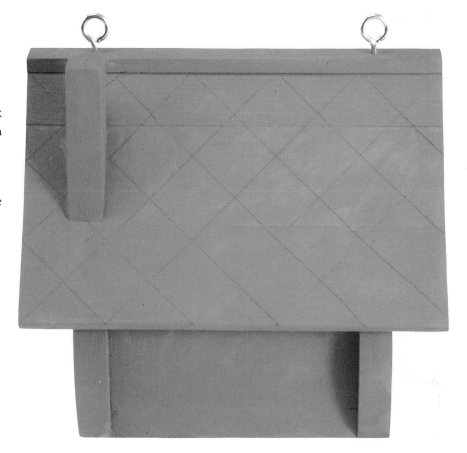

Finished scallops.

Structural Paint

1 Basecoating.

Sand lightly and wipe with a tack cloth. Basecoat the entire house with Raw Sienna and allow to dry.

2 Drawing the Gridwork.

Use a pencil and ruler to divide the roof into equally spaced diagonal rows, then cross the first lines with diagonals going in the opposite direction.

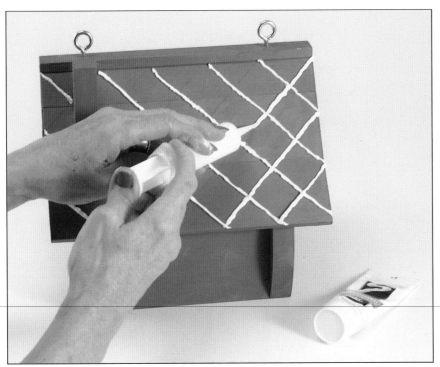

3 Applying Structural Paint.

Squeeze Titanium White structural paint directly from the tube into the 30cc glue injector. Squeeze the injector as you trace over the gridwork pattern lines. Make the trim along the crest of the roof by squeezing a drop of paint, lifting the tube to create a point, then moving to the next space and repeating the process. Draw the windows and doors in the same manner. Using the photo on page 50 as a guide, use Titanium White in the 10cc injector to draw the gridwork on the shutters, the curtains, the windowpanes, the trim above the door and the zigzag pattern on the eaves. Paint the window boxes and chimney mortar Structural Brown with a 10cc tube. Fill a 10cc injector with a little Hooker's Green Hue, then Permanent Green

Press the plunger lightly to release paint along the penciled grid lines, working in one direction at a time.

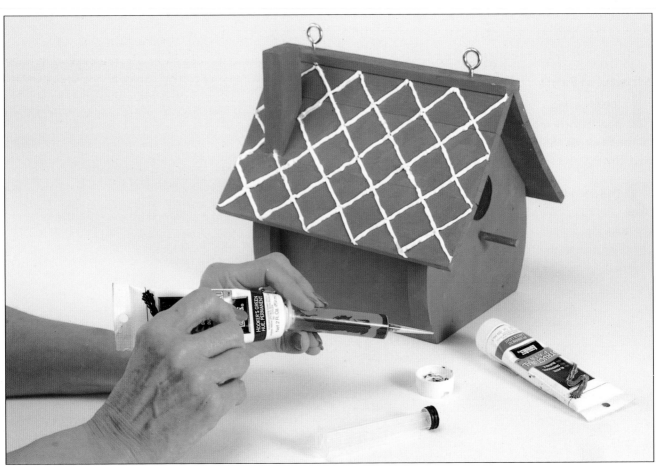

Alternating colors as you fill the injector will create variation in the greenery.

Painting and Decorating Birdhouses

Light, then more Hooker's Green Hue. Alternating colors in the injector creates color variety in the greenery.

Make garland loops under the eaves and across the windows, and paint greenery into the flower boxes. Squeeze a wreath shape around the opening. When the greenery is dry, use a 10cc injector with Naphthol Crimson to make the holly berries and bows on the greenery and flowers in the flower boxes. Use Ivory Black in a 10cc injector to paint the lamps on each side of the door.

Use an overlapping zigzag pattern to create texture and irregular edges in the greenery.

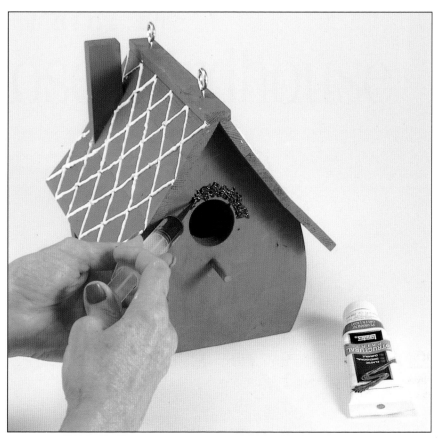

4 Finishing Touches.

When the structural paint is dry, paint the light in the lamps with Cadmium Yellow. Allow to dry, and seal.

Squeeze out dots of Naphthol Crimson for holly berries. Use thicker lines to create the bows.

Bring a taste of the country life into any room of your home with this birdhouse, or hang it outside to add country appeal to a fence post or flower garden. If you'd prefer a weathered gray barn to the red version shown here, simply substitute Slate Grey for the siding and black or barn red for the roof. To give your indoor barn a rustic, aged look, follow the directions for creating a crackled finish given in the Crackled Victorian project.

Paint the
Red Barn Birdhouse

1 Basecoating.
Sand the barn, rounding off corners and sharp edges. Wipe with a tack cloth to remove dust particles. Mix equal amounts of Oxblood and Brandy Wine on your palette. Use a 1″ brush to apply the mixture as a basecoat. Paint the roof and silo with Slate Grey. Allow to dry.

Chicken pattern.

Paint the straw by building layers of yellow, working from dark to light. Trace the siding boards with thinned black on a liner brush.

2 Adding Details.
Draw with a pencil the door, hayloft and guidelines for the siding. With a liner brush and thinned black, paint over the pencil lines for the siding boards and the detail on the doors. Paint the hayloft opening with Lamp Black and the trim around the door with Slate Grey. To make the dots for nails, dip the handle end of a liner brush into Lamp Black, then dot "nails" at the ends of some of the boards.

3 Painting the Straw.
Use the liner brush and thinned paint to draw straw in the hayloft and on the wood block, working from dark to light: Antique Gold, Golden Straw, Cadmium Yellow mixed with white and, finally, Yellow Light mixed with white.

4 Painting the Chicken.
Transfer the chicken pattern to the hayloft, then paint it with Titanium White, using the black background as a shading color. Paint the comb and wattle with True Red and the beak with Cadmium Yellow.

5 Painting the Cutouts.
Basecoat the cow with Titanium White, let dry, then add Lamp Black spots. Paint the milk can Slate Grey. Paint the stripe around the middle of the pig with Titanium White and the rest of the pig Lamp Black, softening slightly between colors.

6 Finishing.
Antique the roof of the barn and the silo with Burnt Sienna, following the directions given in the "Getting Started" section. Antique the milk can with Burnt Umber. When dry, glue the milk can, hay bale, cow and pig to the barn with wood glue, referring to the photo for placement. Seal when dry.

Materials

- barn-shaped birdhouse

DecoArt Americana acrylic paints
- Oxblood
- Brandy Wine
- Slate Grey
- True Red
- Antique Gold
- Golden Straw
- Cadmium Yellow
- Yellow Light
- Lamp Black
- Titanium White

Brushes
- 1″ synthetic flat or 1″ sponge
- no. 4 flat
- no. 10 flat
- no. 0 liner

Miscellaneous
- wooden cutout cow and pig
- miniature milk can
- ½″ × ½″ × 1″ wood block
- wood glue
- pencil
- ruler
- palette
- water container

2 Painting the Tulips.

Use a fine detail brush to paint the small tulips under the eaves and on the awning with Peaches 'n' Cream. Paint the stems and leaves with Hauser Green Medium. Shade the left side of the tulips with a line of Coral Rose. To paint the wooden tulip cutouts, basecoat the flower with Peaches 'n' Cream, then float Coral Rose shading around the edges. Paint the stems and leaves with Hauser Green Medium. Add Yellow Green comma strokes to the leaves and as a highlight line down the middle of the stem.

3 Painting the Rabbit.

Basecoat the rabbit with Titanium White. Tint the ears and nose very lightly with Peaches 'n' Cream. The linework and eyes are done with thinned Lamp Black on a liner brush. Set aside to dry.

4 Adding the Checkerboard Squares.

With Green Mist on the no. 10 brush, paint checkerboard bricks beginning at the top and working down the front and sides. Using the photo as a guide, gradually make the painted bricks lighter and less pronounced toward the bottom and center of the house. They should blend gradually into indistinct washes of color.

5 Painting the Sign.

Draw the lettering on the sign with a pencil to check spacing. Use Peaches 'n' Cream on a liner brush to paint over the pencil lines. Add shadow lines with Burnt Umber. The hearts are painted with Coral Rose. Center and glue the sign just under the perch on the front of the house.

6 Adding Details.

Paint sketchy squares for the lit windows with Golden Straw. Paint the door with Antique Teal. Use Burnt Umber linework to create slightly uneven outlines for the windows and door and to make the hash marks on the front of the house. Glue the cutouts to the house as shown in photo.

7 Painting the Tree.

Use Asphaltum thinned with a little water on a no. 6 brush for the trunk and branches. Create light and dark values by stretching the paint with up-and-down strokes. Strengthen

Steps to build checkerboard pattern.

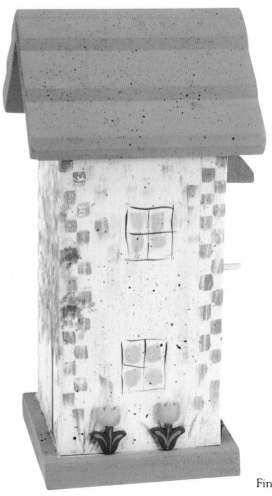

Finished side view.

darks by applying unthinned paint. To paint the foliage, thin Hauser Green Medium with water and use a patting and sliding motion with the corner of the no. 10 brush to suggest leaves. Leave open spaces for a light, airy tree. Use less water to make darker leaves and firm up the final shape of the tree. With the liner brush and thinned Hauser Green Medium, pull up grass strokes around the base of the house. Create dot flowers by dipping the handle of your brush into Peaches 'n' Cream.

8 Finishing.

Spatter the house by dipping a stiff bristle brush into thinned Lamp Black. Holding the bristles 6″ to 8″ from the surface, drag a palette knife across the bristles toward you. When dry, apply several coats of satin-finish varnish. To make the curtains, cut two 2″ squares of fabric. Use heavy white craft glue to attach each piece in gathers under the awning. Cut two ⅝″-wide strips, fold in half lengthwise and glue in place for the tiebacks.

Finished back view.

Paint the tree trunk and branches with thinned Asphaltum, using straight paint for darker textures.

Use a patting-and-sliding motion to apply thinned Hauser Green Medium for the leaves.

Use unthinned Hauser Green Medium to create darker leaves, which will add depth to your tree.

The bright colors of this birdhouse make it an American favorite. Use the illustrations for making masking tape stripes given in the Lighthouse project to complete this quick-and-easy birdhouse.

Painting and Decorating Birdhouses

Paint the
Stars and Stripes Birdhouse

Divide each side into four equal-size stripes.

1 Basecoating.
Sand the birdhouse and stars well. Wipe with a tack cloth to remove dust particles. Basecoat the house with Buttermilk and the roof with Midnight Blue. Paint the star cutouts with Cadmium Yellow Medium.

2 Adding Horizontal Stripes.
To mask off the areas for the front and back stripes, apply one strip of tape across the front of the house, aligning it with the bottom edge of the house. Apply the next strip just above the first one and so on, until the front of the house is covered. Remove the second strip from the bottom and then each alternate strip above it, creating stripes. Paint over the edge of the tape with Buttermilk to seal, and let dry before applying the Pure Red. Several coats may be needed for good coverage. Repeat this process on the back of the house.

3 Adding Vertical Stripes.
To make the vertical stripes on the sides, measure the side from front to back and divide by four. If the house is large, divide by five or six, so that the stripes don't exceed more than 1½" in width. Mark the lines lightly with a pencil and ruler. Lay masking tape along the pencil lines to cover alternate stripes. Paint over the tape edges

with Buttermilk. Let dry, then paint open stripes with Pure Red.

4 Finishing.
Drill holes through the wooden stars and use escutcheon pins to nail them to the roof. You could also attach the stars with wood glue. Seal the entire project.

Materials

- craft store birdhouse

Accent Country Colors acrylic paint
- Pure Red

Apple Barrel acrylic paint
- Midnight Blue

DecoArt Americana acrylic paints
- Cadmium Yellow Medium
- Buttermilk

Brushes
- 1" synthetic flat or 1" sponge
- ½" flat
- no. 4 flat

Miscellaneous
- three 1½" wooden star cutouts
- brass escutcheon pins
- hammer
- drill with ¹⁄₁₆" bit
- pencil
- ruler
- masking tape
- palette
- water container

Adding texture is a great way to make a design come to life. Sculpting flower petals and fruit shapes couldn't be easier than with the new line of decorating pastes available today, and the added dimension actually makes painting easier. Unlike the modeling pastes of the past, decorating paste won't shrink or crack when dry. Try your hand at sculpting strawberries, apples, tulips or any other design that would fit on a birdhouse.

Paint the
Sculpted Sunflowers Birdhouse

Materials for applying sculpting paste.

1 Basecoating.
Sand the house well, rounding off corners and sharp edges. Wipe with a tack cloth to remove dust particles. With a 1″ brush, apply Buttermilk as a basecoat on the front, back and sides of the house. Basecoat the roof and base with Avocado. Allow to dry.

Materials
• craft store birdhouse
• DecoArt Decorating Paste
DecoArt Americana acrylic paint
• Buttermilk
• Avocado
• Hauser Green Light
• Cadmium Yellow
• Antique Gold
• Milk Chocolate
Brushes
• 1″ synthetic flat or 1″ sponge
• no. 4 flat
• no. 10 flat
• no. 1 liner
Miscellaneous
• small, diamond-shaped painting knife
• palette
• water container

2 Sculpting the Petals.

Load the bottom of your painting knife with decorating paste and press it against the top of the first hole. This will form your basic petal shape. Using the pattern at bottom right as a guide, smooth the paste until it resembles a petal. Continue making random individual petals around the circumference of each hole, overlapping some petals and leaving a slight gap between others.

Use the pattern as a guide to apply decorating paste in petal shapes around the openings of the birdhouse.

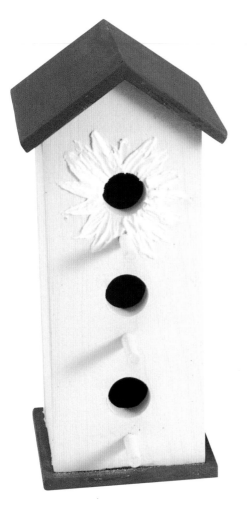

Petals should vary in shape and width.

Allow paste to dry thoroughly before painting.

3 Sculpting the Leaves.

Use the same technique to create three leaves, this time first dabbing your loaded painting knife into a "V" shape, then pressing another pointed shape in the center of the "V." Smooth and shape until you are satisfied with the results, using the photo as a placement guide. Set aside to dry. Drying time is anywhere from four to twelve hours, depending on the thickness of the application and on drying conditions.

Sunflower pattern.

Leaf pattern.

4 Painting the Sunflowers.

Basecoat the petals with Cadmium Yellow. Allow to dry, then shade the petal from the center toward the tip with Antique Gold. Paint the center of the petals (the lip of the holes) with Milk Chocolate, blending it out into the petal slightly.

Basecoat the petals with Cadmium Yellow.

Shade each petal with Antique Gold.

Painting and Decorating Birdhouses

Blend Milk Chocolate around the opening.

5 Painting the Leaves.

Basecoat the leaves with Avocado. Highlight the top edges and along the center vein with Hauser Green Light.

Basecoat the leaves with Avocado.

6 Antiquing.

When the paint is dry, antique the house with a rich brown antiquing glaze or with Burnt Umber oil paint thinned with odorless paint thinner. Apply the antiquing with a brush, then use a soft cloth to remove excess. Leave color stronger around flowers and under the eaves of the roof. Use a soft, dry brush to pull glaze out of small places and soften the edges. Spatter the house by dipping a stiff bristle brush into thinned Burnt Umber. Hold the bristles 6″ to 8″ from the surface, and softly drag a palette knife across the bristles toward you. (Refer to the "Getting Started" section for more information on antiquing and spattering.) Allow to dry, and seal.

No collection would be complete without a birdhouse done with a watermelon motif. It's as American as apple pie and the Fourth of July. This house has a unique shape that would interest the most discerning collector, but great results can be achieved by even an inexperienced painter using the colors and painting technique on any birdhouse shape.

Paint the
Watermelon Birdhouse

1 Sponging the Melon.
To paint the roof of the birdhouse, squeeze Painted Desert, Cottage Rose, Pure Red and Holiday Red onto a palette. Wet a kitchen sponge, then squeeze dry. Pull the corners of the sponge up so it forms a rounded pouf. Dip the center of the sponge into Painted Desert and pat the paint onto the roof, starting at the top and working down to ¾″ from the bottom of the roof. Complete coverage of the red areas won't be achieved until the Pure

Red is applied. Work two or three panels at a time so that the paint stays wet through all the sponging. Next, dip into Cottage Rose and sponge over the first color, allowing it to show through in some places. Repeat with Pure Red. Sponge Holiday Red sparingly over the bottom part of the melon area, still leaving a ¾″ unpainted margin for the rind. Paint the wooden heart cutouts with the same technique and colors, leaving a ½″ band around the edges. Allow to dry.

To paint the melon, sponge on layers of Painted Desert, Cottage Rose, Pure Red and Holiday Red.

2 Painting the Rind.

Paint the ¾" band around the bottom of the roof with Adobe Wash mixed with white. Double load the no. 6 flat brush by stroking one corner through the Adobe Wash mix and the other corner through New Leaf. Stroke the brush back and forth lightly on the palette so that the colors blend in the center of the brush. With the Adobe side on top, paint over the basecoated band so that you achieve a gradual blending from white to light green. Next, dip the brush into water and blot it on a paper towel. Dip one corner of the brush into Pine Needle Green and stroke it back and forth on your palette, spreading the color through only half of the brush. Place the paint-filled side of the brush at the bottom edge of the roof to paint the darkest green value. Several applications may be needed for adequate coverage. Paint the underside of the eaves with Pine Needle Green. Fill in the ½" band on the heart cutouts in the same manner.

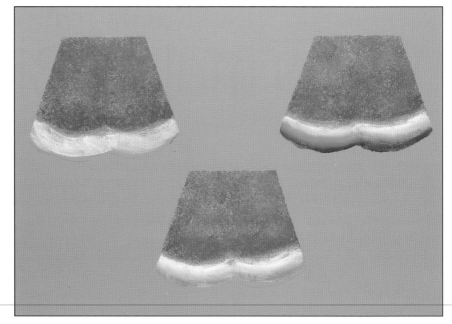

3 Painting the Seeds.

Paint the seeds in a scattered pattern on the roof with Real Black, using the round brush. Highlight the seeds with Adobe Wash. Paint smaller seeds on the heart cutouts.

Painting and Decorating Birdhouses

4 Painting the Base.

Basecoat several sections on the bottom of the house with Pine Needle Green, using the 1″ brush. Use a corner of the brush to liberally apply Hauser Green Light in a randomly edged band along the middle of each section. Add random strokes of Light Jade Green to these bands. Wipe the brush and use the corner to apply tints of Deep Forest Green in the Pine Needle Green areas. Carry small touches of the light stripes into the dark areas. Continue working around the base in this manner.

5 Finishing.

When the paint is dry, apply several coats of satin varnish. Screw the eye-screw into the top of the birdhouse if you intend to hang it. Drill a hole in the "V" at the top edge of each heart. Cut an 18″ length of jute twine and dip the ends into white craft glue. Push the ends of the twine into the holes at the top of the hearts. Set aside to dry. Attach Spanish moss, small berries and flowers to the heart-shaped grapevine wreath with a glue gun. Glue the wreath to the front of the house around the opening. Tie the jute twine with the hearts in a bow on the perch.

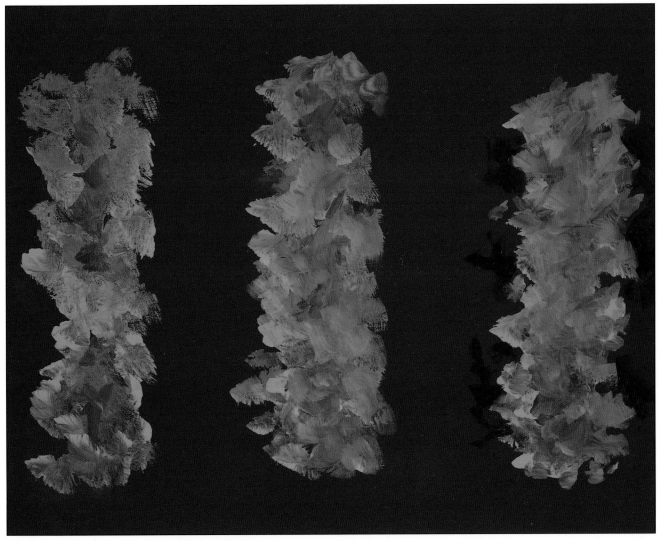

Use the wet-on-wet technique to create uneven, blended bands on the base.

reating a stucco finish is as easy as frosting a cake. And playing with all that texture is great fun! This hacienda would be a nice accent piece in a room with a Southwestern decor, or on a sun-drenched patio.

Paint the
Southwest Pueblo Birdhouse

Raw birdhouse.

Materials

- pueblo-style birdhouse

Liquitex Texture Gel
- Natural Sand

Accent Country Colors acrylic paints
- Peaches 'n' Cream
- Marina Blue
- Sedona Clay

Brushes
- 1″ synthetic flat or 1″ sponge
- no. 4 flat
- liner

Miscellaneous
- painting knife
- miniature table, flower pots and plants
- hot glue gun and glue sticks
- black permanent pen
- palette
- water container

1 Applying the Gel.

Unless the wood piece is very rough, only a light sanding is necessary because the texture gel will cover most of the rough spots. The easiest way to apply the gel is with a small trowel-shaped painting knife. Scoop the gel directly from the jar and apply it to the birdhouse in the same manner that you would use to spread frosting on a cake.

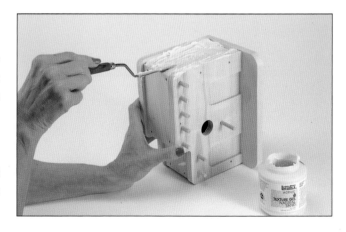

2 Creating Texture.

Slight shrinkage may occur as the gel dries, so use it liberally. Swirl and smooth the gel as you apply it, creating a stuccolike texture. Cover the entire birdhouse, with the exception of the roof support logs and the porch. Allow to dry overnight. The gel will become almost transparent when dry.

Painting and Decorating Birdhouses

Basecoat over the dry texture gel, being sure to work the paint into hard-to-reach places.

3 Painting.

Stain the roof support beams with a dark wood stain, or with Burnt Umber oil paint, thinned with odorless thinner. Mix approximately one part Sedona Clay to four parts Peaches 'n' Cream. Paint the stuccoed parts of the house with this mixture. Paint the doors with Marine Blue and the porch with Sedona Clay.

4 Finishing.

Use a liner brush with Burnt Umber oil paint to draw a plank pattern on the doors. Draw vertical lines for the planks and horizontal lines for the crossboards. Use thinner on the chisel edge of a flat brush to remove the lines inside the horizontal planks. Pull shading from the linework. Use a black permanent pen to draw the doorknob. Seal the entire project. When dry, use a hot glue gun to decorate the porch with miniature plants and accessories from the dollhouse section of your local hobby or craft store.

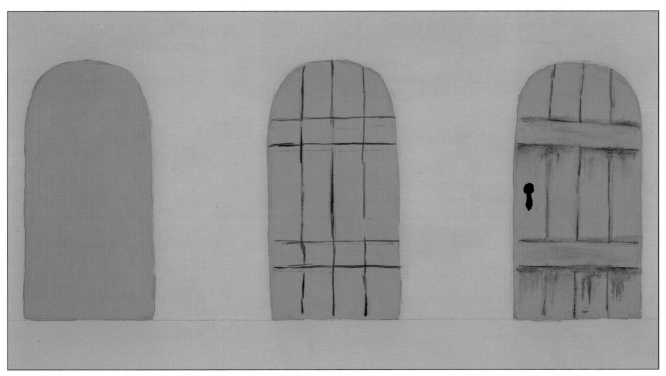

Paint the doors Marina Blue and add a plank pattern with Burnt Umber oil paint.

These birdhouses have an old-fashioned patriotic appeal that's as irresistible as apple pie. Included in this project are instructions to create mirror-image bookends by cutting a fence post to size. If you don't have the tools or desire to build your own bookends, buy two identical ready-made birdhouses and paint them as described, or use the painting techniques shown to decorate a single birdhouse to hang outdoors.

Paint the
Patriotic Bookends
Birdhouses

Star stencil pattern.

1 Making the Bookends.

Cut the post to size, making two pieces that are flat on one end and cut at an angle on the other. They can be any height. The bookends in the sample are 3½″ high on one side and 7¼″ on the other. To make the roof, cut two pieces, measuring 3¾″ × 6½″, from the ¼″-thick wood. Attach the roof piece to the house with nails or wood glue. Drill a 1″ hole in the front center for the nest, and a ¼″ hole for the perch. Glue a dowel rod into the hole for the perch.

2 Basecoating.

Sand edges to create a worn, primitive look, then wipe with tack cloth. Basecoat the roofs with Uniform Blue and the houses and star cutouts with Antique White.

3 Adding Stripes.

When dry, mark off the width of the stripes with a pencil. With your ¾″ (or smaller if necessary) brush loaded with Brandy Wine, pull the stripes from top to bottom in even lines.

4 Stenciling.

Trace the star patterns onto lightweight cardboard. Use a craft knife to cut out star shapes, keeping corners sharp and neat. Position the stencil on the roof and use masking tape to hold it securely in place. Dip the stencil brush into Antique White. Pat it on the palette repeatedly to remove excess paint—stenciling is done with an almost dry brush. Begin patting the brush on the edge of the cardboard, then work gradually with a stippling motion out onto the design area until it is lightly covered. Starting on the cardboard ensures you won't place a dark blob of color on your surface each time you reload the brush.

5 Antiquing.

When your paint is dry, apply a mixture of Burnt Umber and Raw Umber, thinned with odorless thinner, or antiquing glaze over the entire house and star cutouts. Wipe away excess with a soft cloth. Set aside to dry.

6 Spattering.

To spatter the bookends and stars, use your stencil brush loaded with slightly thinned paint. Hold the brush 6″ to 8″ from the bookend and pull a palette knife lightly across the bristles toward you. Spatter first with Williamsburg Blue, then Lamp Black, then the antiquing medium.

7 Finishing.

Use a ¹⁄₁₆″ bit to drill a hole in the star cutouts. Use brass upholstery tacks to attach the star cutouts to the front of the bookends. Seal the entire project. When dry, glue a bit of Spanish moss into the nest openings.

Materials

- two identical ready-made wooden birdhouses
- *or* wooden fence post, approximately 3″ × 4″ diameter
- ¼″-thick piece of wood
- two 2″-long, ¼″-thick dowel rods

DecoArt Americana acrylic paint
- Antique White
- Brandy Wine
- Uniform Blue
- Williamsburg Blue
- Lamp Black

Brushes
- ¾″ synthetic flat or 1″ sponge
- no. 6 flat
- stencil brush

Miscellaneous
- two star-shaped wooden cutouts
- sheet of thin cardboard or shirt board
- two brass upholstery tacks
- band saw
- hammer and small nails
- wood glue
- pencil
- masking tape
- craft knife
- drill with 1″, ¼″ and ¹⁄₁₆″ bits
- Spanish moss
- palette and water container

You'll be amazed at the character you can give a plain, mass-produced birdhouse just by adding texture with commercial patching compounds (available at most home improvement stores). In this project you'll turn an ordinary birdhouse into a charming flower-covered cottage that looks as if it came straight from the English countryside.

Paint the
Brick and Stucco
Cottage Birdhouse

1 Painting the Bricks.
Paint the Popsicle sticks with Georgia Clay, then randomly brush them with tints of Brandy Wine and Uniform Blue, adding only enough color variation to give a bricklike appearance. Allow to dry.

Raw house and materials.

Materials

- craft store birdhouse

DecoArt Americana acrylic paints
- Sand
- Midnite Green
- Hauser Green Dark
- Avocado
- Yellow Green
- Crimson Tide
- Cherry Red
- Coral Rose
- Uniform Blue
- Olde Gold
- Georgia Clay
- Brandy Wine

Brushes
- 1″ synthetic flat or 1″ sponge
- no. 4 synthetic flat
- no. 8 flat
- bristle fan

Miscellaneous
- premixed concrete and mortar patch
- popcorn ceiling patch
- eight or nine Popsicle sticks
- trowel-shaped painting knife
- craft knife or pruning shears
- palette
- water container

2 Cutting the Bricks.

Use a craft knife or pruning shears to cut the sticks into 1″ "bricks." Touch up the raw ends with Georgia Clay. Set aside.

3 Applying Texture.

No sanding is necessary, as the concrete and mortar patch will cover any rough spots. Apply the mortar patch material to all sides of the house as you would apply plaster to a wall, using a small, trowel-shaped painting knife. Pat it on, then spread it as evenly as possible with the knife. Leave a 1″ margin untouched all around the bottom of the house.

Painting and Decorating Birdhouses

4 Adding Bricks.
While the mortar is still wet, push a few groups of "bricks" into it, staggering placement and number of bricks used in each area. Use the photo as a placement guide.

5 Covering the Roof.
Spread a thick layer of mortar patch over the roof, including the eaves and perch overhang. (The eaves and perch overhang were done in a later step in the demo pictures.)

6 Thatching the Roof.

While the roof is still wet, use the edge of the painting knife to press gently into the mortar to create the appearance of thatching. Brush gentle downward strokes over the thatching with a stiff bristle fan brush to smooth it slightly. Use the same steps to texture the perch overhang.

Create "thatching" by pressing the edge of the knife gently into the mortar.

Brush soft downward strokes over the thatching pattern to smooth the mortar slightly.

Painting and Decorating Birdhouses

7 Creating the Foliage.

To make the vines and flowers, use the tip of the painting knife to dab popcorn ceiling patch into the untouched area around the bottom of the birdhouse. Pull vines of different heights up into the mortar patch area. Allow to dry.

8 Basecoating.

Paint the sides of the house with Sand, being careful when painting around the bricks. Use a wet-on-wet technique to paint the greenery, working from dark to light. Start by dabbing on Midnite Green, paying special attention to the lower, thicker areas of the foliage.

9 Painting the Foliage.

While the Midnite Green is still wet, dab in Hauser Green Dark, then Avocado, and finally Yellow Green, being sure to let some of each color show through.

Cover more of the foliage area with Hauser Green Dark.

Dab on Avocado. Almost all the foliage area should be covered by now.

Painting and Decorating Birdhouses

10 Painting the Flowers.
When the green is thoroughly dry, paint the flowers in the same manner, starting with random dots of Crimson Tide.

11 Finishing the Flowers.

Touch in areas of Cherry Red and Coral Rose, especially concentrating on the tops and vines of the foliage. Because acrylic paint darkens as it dries, you may need to retouch the brightest greens and pinks.

Allow the foliage to dry, then retouch highlights if necessary.

12 Painting the Thatch.

Paint the roof and perch overhang with Olde Gold. Allow to dry.

Be sure to paint the underside of the eaves.

13 **Antiquing the Roof.**
To add depth and bring out the texture of the thatching, antique the roof according to the instructions given in the "Getting Started" section. Be sure to work the antiquing glaze down into the crevasses and shadowed overhangs with a brush. Wipe lightly with a soft cloth to remove excess stain.

Apply antiquing glaze to the thatched areas.

Wipe off excess glaze with a soft cloth.

14 Creating Highlights.

To lighten some of the flat areas of the roof, wipe off more of the antiquing glaze with a brush dipped in odorless thinner. When dry, finish the entire house with an indoor/outdoor matte varnish.

Antiquing the roof adds depth to the shadowed areas and brings out the coarse texture of the thatch.

C hange a ready-made birdhouse into a custom design by adding a few simple cuts of
wood. The bottom ark pieces and the rainbow were cut and added to a craft store birdhouse.
Draw an ark design to fit the birdhouses available
in your area, or enlarge the pattern shown on page
107 on a copier by 200 percent.

Paint the
Noah's Ark Birdhouse

1 **Cutting the Wood Pieces.**
Draw a pattern like the one shown to cut the rainbow-shaped piece from ¼" plywood. Drill a hole in each end of the rainbow and near the bottom of each side of the roof. Cut two curved pieces for the bottom of the ark from ½" white pine and nail them to the birdhouse, using the photo as a guide.

2 **Basecoating.**
Basecoat the ark sides with Adobe Wash, the roof with Barn Red and the bottom with Tumbleweed. Paint the rainbow white. Paint the awning with Stoneware Blue. When dry, sand paint from the edges to create an aged look.

Materials

- craft store birdhouse
- ¼" plywood
- ½" white pine
- two jumbo craft sticks

Accent Country Colors acrylic paints
- Adobe Wash
- Barn Red
- Stoneware Blue
- Tumbleweed
- Pure Yellow
- True Orange
- Pure Red
- Pure Blue
- Real Black
- Burnt Umber
- Light Peaches 'n' Cream
- White

Delta Ceramcoat acrylic paint
- Jubilee Green

Brushes
- 1" synthetic flat or 1" sponge
- no. 4 flat
- no. 8 flat
- no. 1 liner

Miscellaneous
- band saw
- wood glue
- hammer
- nails
- two brass escutcheon pins
- drill with ¹⁄₁₆" bit
- jute twine
- pencil
- 19-gauge wire
- wire cutters
- black permanent pen
- palette
- water container

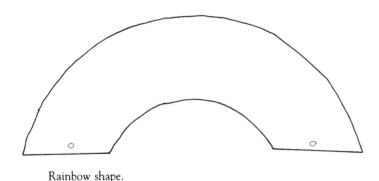

Rainbow shape.

Ark shape.

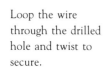

Loop the wire
through the drilled
hole and twist to
secure.

3 Painting the Rainbow.
To paint the rainbow, use the pencil to lightly divide the rainbow into five stripes. Paint the bottom stripe with Pure Yellow, the next stripe with True Orange, then Pure Red, then Jubilee Green, and finally the last stripe with Pure Blue.

4 Antiquing.
Antique the ark and rainbow by applying to all pieces antiquing glaze or Burnt Umber oil paint thinned with odorless thinner. Wipe away excess with a soft cloth. Seal when dry.

5 Attaching the Wire.
Cut a 36″ length of wire. Thread one end through the drilled hole in the roof. Bring it up to form a loop, and wrap it around itself above the hole to hold the end securely.

6 Curling the Wire.
Move up the wire slightly and wrap it several times around a pencil to curl it, then thread it through one end of the rainbow. Add more curls in the wire and thread it through the other side of the roof and attach as you did in step 5.

To curl the wire, wrap it around a pencil several times.

Painting and Decorating Birdhouses

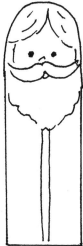

Noah pattern.

7 Painting Noah.

Cut a 2½″ end piece from one craft stick. Paint the face area with Light Peaches 'n' Cream. Paint the cloak with Burnt Umber and add a stripe of Stoneware Blue down the front. Underpaint the hair and beard with a mixture of Real Black and Adobe Wash. Overstroke with Adobe Wash on the liner brush. Paint a fine line for the top of the nose with Barn Red. Make black dots for the eyes with the handle end of a small brush or with a permanent pen.

8 Making the Sign.

Cut a 1¾″ rectangular piece from the other jumbo craft stick. Basecoat the piece with Adobe Wash and outline the edge with Barn Red. When dry, lightly write in pencil "Noah & Co." on the sign to check spacing, then ink over the pencil lines with a permanent pen.

9 Finishing Touches.

Tie one strand of jute around Noah for a belt. Glue Noah in place on the ark. Use brass escutcheon pins to tack the sign to the ark.

Steps to paint Noah.

I t's easy and fun to turn a plain birdhouse of any style into a rustic log cabin by using concrete patch, hand-made or dollhouse shake shingles and twig-size logs. This birdhouse would be right at home hung from a pine tree at a cabin retreat or displayed on the mantel of an old stone fireplace.

Decorate the
Log Cabin Birdhouse

Raw birdhouse and supplies.

1 Making Your Own Shingles.

Although you may prefer the convenience of buying ready-made dollhouse shingles, cutting your own shingles is a quick and easy process, and will cost you much less than buying precut shingles. To cut your own shingles, select cedar with a straight, even grain. Decide on the size of each shingle. The shingles used here are 5⁄8" wide by 1" long. Cut the cedar across the grain to the desired size. Secure the wood in a vise, and use a wood chisel to chip the shingles from the wood piece.

2 Cutting the Logs.

To make the logs, select sticks that are as straight as possible. Trim away knobs and side branches. Measure each twig against the section of the house it will cover and mark the appropriate length with a pencil, allowing ½″ excess so that the sticks will overlap each other at the corners. With the pruning shears or saw, cut enough twigs to space evenly over the sides, back and front of the house.

If your birdhouse has windows or an opening, cut shorter sticks to frame the openings and the door.

Measure sticks to fit the sides of the birdhouse, allowing ½″ extra for corners.

Trim sticks with pruning shears.

Cut shorter sticks for around the windows and doors.

3 Applying the Mortar.

Spread the mortar over one side of the house at a time. You may want to begin on the back of the birdhouse so that you can get a feel for working with the materials before you move to a more prominent section. Use a painting knife or small trowel to spread mortar patch on the wall of the house. The mortar should be about ¼″ thick so that it will hold the logs when they are pressed into it.

4 Pressing in the Logs.

Gently push each log into the wet mortar patch. Leave one stick-width between each log. When you add sticks to the other sides, the placement of logs and spaces will alternate so that the logs overlap each other at the corners rather than join in continuous lines.

5 Applying Mortar Around the Opening.

Once you've mastered the technique, move to the sides and then the front of the birdhouse. Cover the surface with mortar patch. Be sure to spread mortar into the opening, smoothing it around the hole.

6 Framing the Window.
Using the shorter logs, frame the opening first, allowing the smaller top and bottom sticks to sit inside the side frames.

7 Adding a Door.
Press a rectangular piece of wood into the mortar for a door. The sample uses a 1″ × 3″ piece; cut your door piece to fit proportionally with the size of your house. The door piece should appear a little too skinny. Adding the stick frame will increase its size. If your wood piece is too large, it will look out of proportion once the frame is added.

8 Finishing the Logs.
Use three sticks to frame the door. Set the top stick outside the side pieces as shown. Cut sticks to fit between the door and window, aligning the first short log with the bottom of the window frame. Fill in the front and remaining sides, alternating sticks as shown.

To make the door frame, press shorter sticks into the mortar on three sides.

Cut shorter logs to fit between the window and door.

Painting and Decorating Birdhouses

9 Laying the First Row of Shingles.

Squeeze a line of glue along the bottom edge of the roof. Press the first row of shingles into place along the glue line, allowing them to overhang the roof slightly, but creating an even bottom edge.

Decorate the Log Cabin Birdhouse

10 Finishing the Shingles.

Squeeze a line of glue directly onto the top edge of the first row of shingles and a second line onto the roof above the finished row. Starting with a very narrow shingle, press the second row in place, overlapping the bottom edge of the second row onto the top edge of the first row. Repeat this process until the entire roof is covered, using a full-size shingle to start the next row, then alternating with a narrow shingle for the next row, and so on. This will vary the pattern of shingles so that you don't end up with even vertical lines of shingles. Allow a few of the shingles to extend slightly below the rest to prevent the horizontal lines from becoming too precise. To give the top a finished look, lay the final row on either side of the roof with the shingles running horizontally. Stain the shingles and door with walnut stain, and seal when dry. You can add hinges and a knob on the door with a black permanent pen if you wish.

11 Covering the Chimney.

Apply mortar patch to the chimney, spreading it into gaps between the shingles and chimney piece.

12 Finishing.

Press small rocks or pieces of gravel into the wet mortar on the chimney. Try to space the rocks evenly over the chimney, without creating a definite pattern. Use smaller rocks as you reach the top of the chimney. Allow to dry and set completely.

Choose stones with a variety of shapes and sizes, placing them in a random pattern.

Gallery

Vine-Covered Cottage

Even the plainest birdhouse can be made special with the addition of a few simple wooden cutouts. You'll need a jigsaw or band saw for cutting the leaf and sunflower shapes (or a willing friend with a workshop). Attach the leaves with curled wire as shown in the Noah's Ark project. Use a casual, "not quite within the lines" painting technique to achieve the primitive charm of this birdhouse.

Painting and Decorating Birdhouses

Beeline Diner
Just like the Noah's Ark project, adding a simple cut of wood converted this craft store
birdhouse into a custom design. Here, a hot-pink wooden awning was added to complete
the look of a '50s roadside diner.

Sunflower

No birdhouse shape is limited to one end result. This octagonal shape was also used for the watermelon birdhouse. Many of the same wet-on-wet painting techniques were used to create both projects.

Decoupage Cottage

Decoupage is a wonderful way to add an intricate design to an entire surface without actually painting it. While only a section of a design was applied to the surface in the teapot project, in this example, wrapping paper was applied to cover the sides completely.

Cowboy Boot

If you get a kick out of watching the birds, this is the house for you. Made from an old cowboy boot, it has a charm and humor about it that would add fun to any patio or yard. Many hollow everyday objects can be recycled into creative birdhouses.

Painting and Decorating Birdhouses

Birdhouse Wreath
Perfect for the birdhouse collector with limited space, scale down any of the painting techniques from the full-size projects to decorate your miniature houses.

List of Suppliers

The raw birdhouses used in this book were purchased from the following manufacturers. If your local craft and hobby stores don't carry the design you're looking for, contact these companies for more information.

Walnut Hollow
(800) 950-5101

Woodcraft products available nationwide at leading craft and department stores.

Add Your Touch
P.O. Box 570
Ripon, WI 54971
(414) 748-6777

A complete mail-order line of kit and assembled wooden birdhouses, also available at craft stores.

Something Different
P.O. Box 52174
Tulsa, OK 74152

Mail-order glue injectors (for structural paint) and handmade wooden birdhouses shown on pages 30, 69, 84 and 122.

Index